HOW TO DRAW YOUR OWN GRAPHIC NOVEL

DRAWING THE VILLAINS
IN YOUR GRAPHIC NOVEL

FRANK LEE

PowerKiDS press.

New York

Published in 2012 by The Rosen Publishing Group, Inc.

29 East 21st Street, New York, NY 10010

Text and Illustrations: Frank Lee with Jim Hansen

Editors: Joe Harris and Kate Overy

U.S. Editor: Kara Murray

Design: Andrew Easton

Cover Design: Andrew Easton

Library of Congress Cataloging-in-Publication Data

Lee, Frank, 1980–

Drawing the villains in your graphic novel / by Frank Lee.

    p. cm. —— (How to draw your own graphic novel)

Includes index.

ISBN 978-1-4488-6433-1 (library binding) —— ISBN 978-1-4488-6449-2 (pbk.) ——

ISBN 978-1-4488-6450-8 (6-pack)

1. Villains in art—Juvenile literature. 2. Figure drawing—Technique—Juvenile literature. 3. Comic books, strips,

etc.—Technique—Juvenile literature. I. Title.

NC825.V54L44 2012

741.5′1—dc23

                              2011026827

Printed in China

SL002070US

CPSIA Compliance Information: Batch #AW2102PK: For Further Information contact Rosen Publishing, New York, New York at 1-800-237-9932

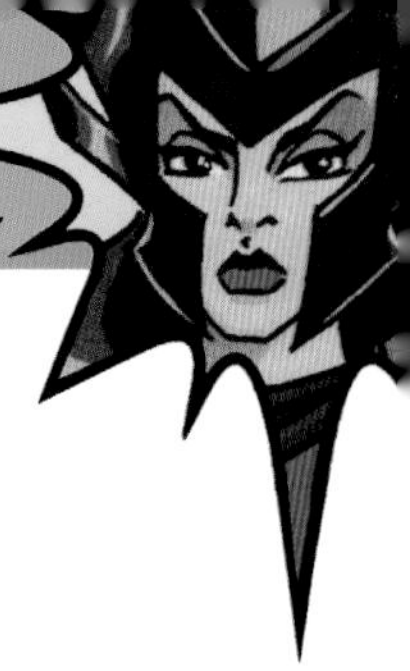

CONTENTS

DRAWING TOOLS

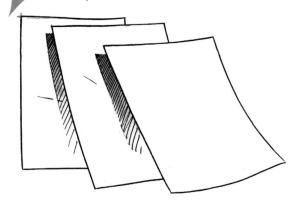

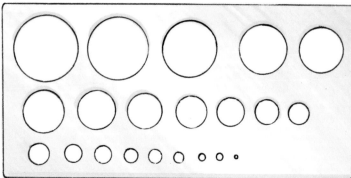

CIRCLE TEMPLATE

This is very useful for drawing small circles.

LAYOUT PAPER

Most professional illustrators use cheaper paper for basic layouts and practice sketches before they get around to the more serious task of producing a masterpiece on more costly paper. It's a good idea to buy some plain paper from a stationery shop for all of your practice sketches. Go for the least expensive kind.

DRAWING PAPER

This is a heavy-duty, high-quality paper, ideal for your final version. You don't have to buy the most expensive brand. Most decent art or craft shops stock their own brand or a student brand and, unless you're thinking of turning professional, these will do fine.

WATERCOLOR PAPER

This paper is made from 100 percent cotton and is much higher quality than wood-based papers. Most art shops stock a large range of weights and sizes. Paper that is 140 pounds (300 g/m) should be fine.

FRENCH CURVES

These are available in a few shapes and sizes and are useful for drawing curves.

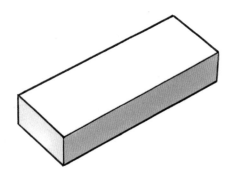

ERASER

There are three main types of eraser: rubber, plastic, and putty. Try all three to see which kind you prefer.

PENCILS

It's best not to cut corners on quality here. Get a good range of graphite (lead) pencils ranging from soft (#1) to hard (#4).

Hard lead lasts longer and leaves less graphite on the paper. Soft lead leaves more lead on the paper and wears down more quickly. Every artist has their personal preference, but #3 pencils are a good medium range to start out with until you find your favorite.

Spend some time drawing with each weight of pencil and get used to their different qualities. Another good product to try is the mechanical pencil. These are available in a range of lead thicknesses, 0.5 mm being a good medium range. These pencils are very good for fine detail work.

PENS

There is a large range of good-quality pens on the market these days and all will do a decent job of inking. It's important to experiment with different pens to determine which you are most comfortable using.

You may find that you end up using a combination of pens to produce your finished artwork. Remember to use a pen that has waterproof ink if you want to color your illustration with a watercolor or ink wash. It's a good idea to use one of these anyway. There's nothing worse than having your nicely inked drawing ruined by an accidental drop of water!

BRUSHES

Some artists like to use a fine brush for inking linework. This takes a bit more practice and patience to master, but the results can be very satisfying. If you want to try your hand at brushwork, you will definitely need to get some good-quality sable brushes.

MARKERS

These are very versatile pens and, with practice, can give pleasing results.

INKS

With the dawn of computers and digital illustration, materials such as inks have become a bit obscure, so you may have to look harder for these. Most good art and craft shops should stock them, though.

HOW TO MAKE A MONSTER

Everyone loves a good bad guy! A strong villain will be essential for creating drama in your graphic novel. When you create your hero's enemy, ask yourself: what is his motivation? Does he crave money or power? Is he evil, crazy, or just misguided? What are his powers and abilities? For a villain to rise up the ranks, he must be a real threat to your hero. Let your imagination run wild!

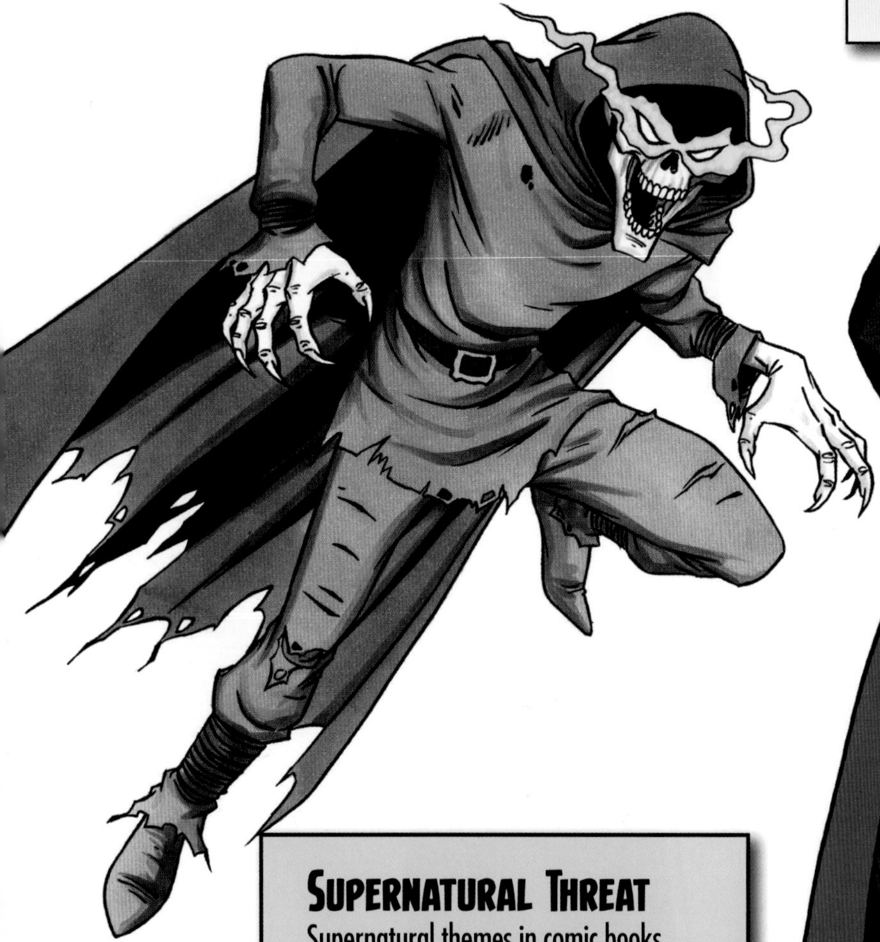

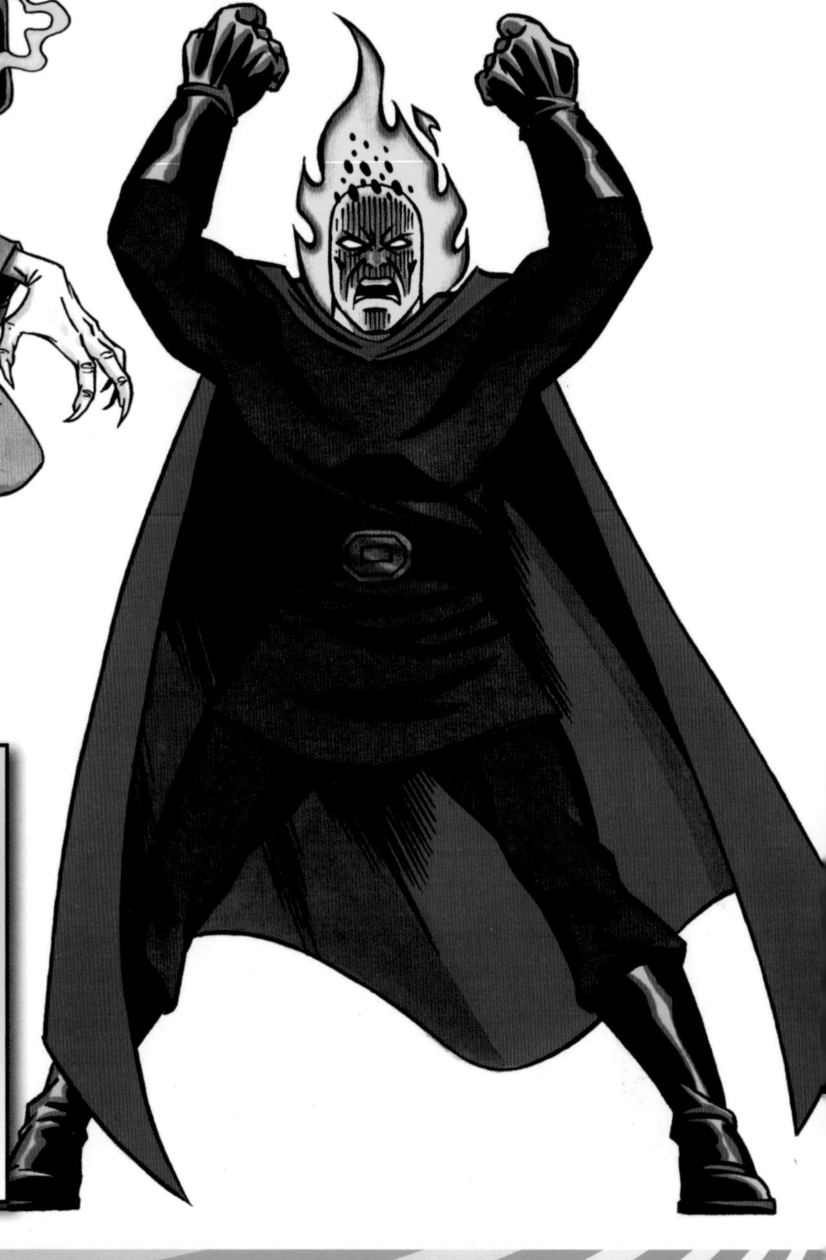

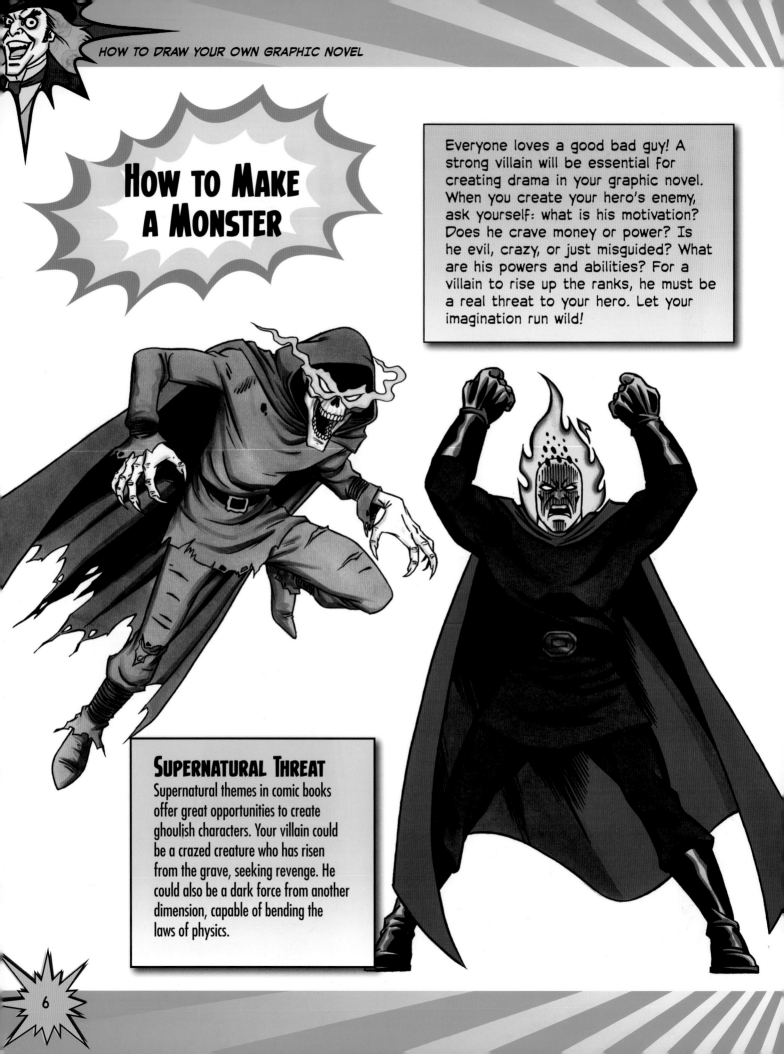

SUPERNATURAL THREAT

Supernatural themes in comic books offer great opportunities to create ghoulish characters. Your villain could be a crazed creature who has risen from the grave, seeking revenge. He could also be a dark force from another dimension, capable of bending the laws of physics.

VAMPIRE

The undead, especially vampires, are a popular choice for writers of horror comics. Vampire abilities include superhuman strength, enhanced speed, and the ability to regenerate. These powers make them very tricky opponents to defeat.

CRAZED MAGICIAN

Your villain could be an evil magician with uncanny powers. Such an illusionist could create many mind-bending obstacles for your hero. Her skills might include telepathy, teleportation, energy blasts, and the creation of protective force fields.

DRAGON

Villains aren't always the shape and size of humans. You might want to create a massive monster for your story. Your hero's source of danger could be a great dragon, an ancient creature that has been summoned to destroy the planet after centuries of slumber.

GOBLINS

Your supervillain might need some accomplices to carry out his master plan. Goblins and elves can add moments of humor to a story as well as horror and suspense. Although diminutive in size and easily overpowered in a fair fight, their sly, cunning abilities are often underestimated by the hero.

MUSCULAR MONSTER

Huge, supercharged behemoths that rampage through the story, causing mayhem and destruction, are always welcome in comic books. They guarantee explosive action and good battle scenes for the hero.

WICKED QUEEN

You could give your story a medieval setting and create a kingdom ruled by an evil, powerful king or queen.

ESCAPED CONVICT

A violent convict who has escaped from prison makes a good villain. This guy's raw strength and cold-blooded nature make him a danger to society. Your villain does not have to be physically strong, though, a brilliant mind can be harder to defeat.

905-702-B

VICTORIAN VILLAIN

You could give your story a historical setting and explore another era. Think of the dark drama you could create in the smoky, lamplit streets of Victorian London, for example. You'll need to research your costumes and scenery to get the atmosphere right.

SINISTER CLOWN

Clowns, puppets, and mannequins are often used to great dramatic effect in tales of suspense and horror. Heavy makeup and oversized, colorful costumes mask the true emotions and intentions of the performer, which can be unnerving. The brightly painted, jolly face of a clown can suddenly take on a sinister appearance when it masks the face of a fiend.

MAD SCIENTIST

Crazy professors spend their time mixing lethal chemicals, designing deadly weapons, or creating superhuman creatures. They can be fun to build into your story. What will your mad scientist unleash upon an unsuspecting world?

CREATING A REALISTIC VILLAIN

TOUGH GUY TONY

In this book you'll learn how to draw a variety of different villains. You could choose to adapt and develop one of these figures to create a brand new enemy for your hero.

STEP 1

Start by drawing a stick figure, then add construction shapes to flesh him out.

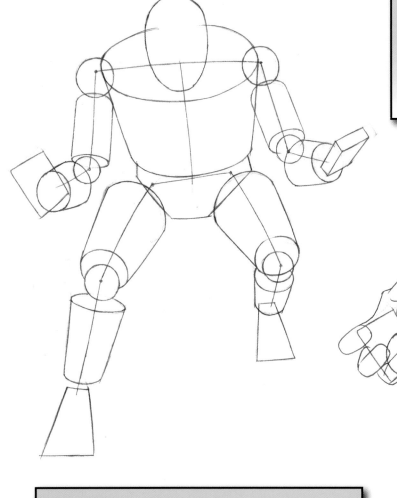

STEP 2

Draw around the shapes to create an outline, then add the face. Give him a mean expression and gritted teeth, as if he's snarling.

STEP 4

Finish your pencil drawing by adding broken chains and shackles. Add some shading, blocking in the areas that will be inked solidly in black.

STEP 3

Remove your working lines and clean up your pencil drawing. Start adding detail, such as the convict's standard-issue prison uniform.

905-702-B

STEP 5
Carefully following your
pencil lines, ink your
drawing to give it more
power and impact.

STEP 6

Coloring this character is very simple as you only need three colors; peach for the skin tones, blue for the uniform, and dark gray for the chains and boots.

CREATING A FANTASY VILLAIN

MAJESTRA

When you are creating a fantasy character, the only limit is your imagination. This malicious monarch has a design that could be recognized even in silhouette.

STEP 1

Build the figure using the stick frame and construction shapes. This warrior queen has a commanding pose.

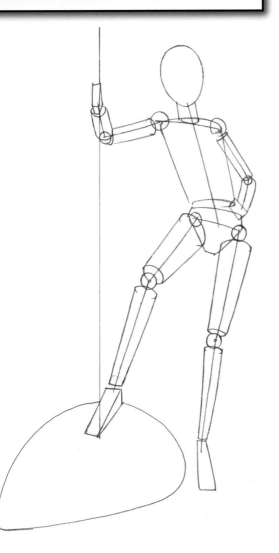

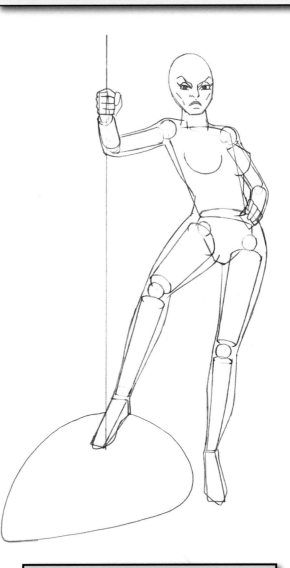

STEP 2

Refine the body shape by outlining around the construction shapes. Give the queen a tough, scornful expression.

STEP 3

Erase your construction shapes and start adding detail. Draw the armor and sword. Jagged edges make them look aggressive. Draw the skull of the slain beast on which she is resting her foot.

STEP 4

Finish the pencil drawing by adding final details and shading.

STEP 5
Carefully ink over
your pencil drawing.

STEP 6

Finally, add color to your drawing. For a dramatic effect we have chosen red for the wicked queen's clothing and black for her boots, crown, and hair. Shades of blue are used to create a shiny effect on her hair and boots. Layers of gray are shaded on top of the red base to add depth. Gray and earthy tones are used to color the skull.

CREATING A MAD SCIENTIST

DOC PARADOX
No rogue's gallery would be complete without a mad scientist character. This unhinged genius is constantly inventing new threats for your hero.

STEP 1
Start to draw the figure using a stick frame. Add construction shapes to the frame.

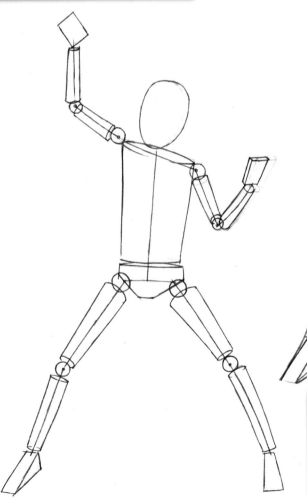

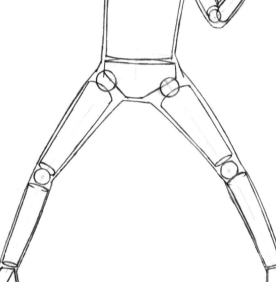

STEP 2
Draw the face and hair. Give this character an exaggerated expression.

STEP 3
Clean up your pencil work and draw his clothing. We've chosen a classic lab coat for this nutty professor. Draw the bubbling potion he is holding.

STEP 4
Finalize your pencil drawing by adding shading, to prepare it for inking.

STEP 5
Ink your pencil drawing by faithfully going over your pencil work.

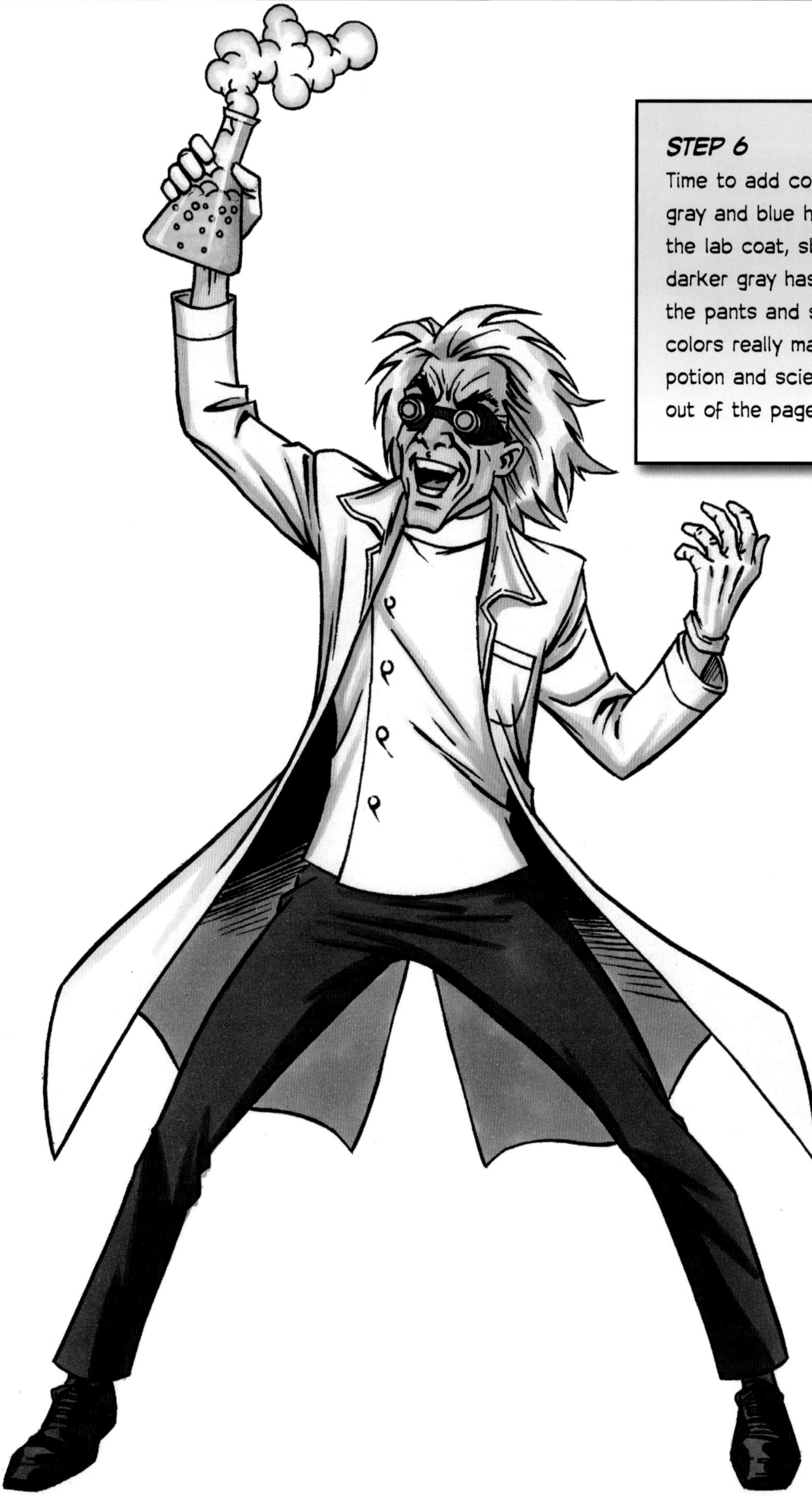

STEP 6

Time to add color! Shades of light gray and blue have been used for the lab coat, shirt, and hair. A darker gray has been applied to the pants and shoes. These simple colors really make the bright green potion and scientist's goggles pop out of the page!

ANIMATED VILLAINS

THE BARBAROUS BRUTE

Why not experiment with different art styles? The next two characters have a slick, stylized look. You may recognize this streamlined design from TV superhero animations.

STEP 1

Start the figure with a frame and simple construction shapes.

STEP 2

This guy stands six heads high and is just as wide. By bulking up his muscles and shrinking his head as compared with his shoulders, we get a troublemaker that no hero would want to tangle with.

STEP 3
With an animated character, you can carry some of the simple curves and lines from your initial construction shapes right through to the final pencils.

STEP 4
Secondary colors like green and purple are classic shades for comic book supervillains. They make for a weirder, less friendly palette than the red, blue, and yellow often worn by heroes.

THE JADE ASSASSIN
This female character also has the clean, simple lines of an animated character. However, rather than being bulky and squat, she is tall and elegant.

STEP 1
Start with a simple stick figure, using rounded shapes to mark out her head, chest, hips, and feet.

STEP 2
Her eyes are slightly narrower and sharper edged.

STEP 3

Always put in more practice on the face. Your character has to look feminine, in both body and face, even if you want her to be a villain.

STEP 4

To make her hair look sleek and glossy, use a light blue highlight. Note the shadow that her sword casts across her legs.

ARCHVILLAINS

DEADLY DEMON
Does your villain serve a more powerful master? Perhaps he follows the orders of a demon, the very embodiment of evil.

MAFIA BOSS
Mafia bosses are ruthless, powerful characters. Gangsters make great archvillains and are characters we love to hate.

GRAND HIGH NINJA

A super-powered martial artist is a formidable opponent for any hero.

WICKED WARLORD

A crazy military mastermind with evil ambitions could command the evil forces in your story.

GLOSSARY

archvillain (AHRCH-vih-lun) A hero's or a heroine's greatest enemy in a story, such as the Joker in D.C. Comics' Batman stories.

construction shapes (Kun-STRUK-shun SHAYPS) Shapes, such as blocks and balls, which are drawn over a sticklike figure to make it more three-dimensional.

horror comics (HOHR-ur KO-miks) A type of comic in which the story and graphics are intended to frighten its readers.

layouts (LAY-owts) Sketches that show where items, such as figures and words, will be positioned on each page.

Mafia (MAH-fee-uh) A secret criminal organization, originally from Italy, which is well known for having ruthless bosses.

ninja (NIN-juh) A person (or creature) trained in martial arts or a Japanese warrior.

realistic (ree-uh-LIS-tik) Similar to real life rather than imaginary.

secondary colors (SEH-kun-der-ee KUH-lurz) Colors made by mixing two primary colors, such as green, which is made by mixing yellow and blue.

stick figure (STIK FIH-gyur) A simple drawing of a figure using sticks and circles.

supernatural (soo-per-NA-chu-rul) Anything that lies beyond the natural world and that cannot be explained by science, such as ghosts.

Further Reading

Besel, Jennifer M. *The Captivating, Creative, Unusual History of Comic Books.* Unusual Histories. Mankato, MN: Capstone Press, 2010.

Dakin, Glenn. *Disney Villains: The Essential Guide.* DK Essential Guides. New York: DK Children, 2004.

DeFalco, Tom. *Spider-Girl,* volume 12: The Games Villains Play. Marvel Adventures Spider-Girl Digest. New York: Marvel 2010.

Hitch, Bryan. *Bryan Hitch's Ultimate Comics Studio.* New York: Impact, 2010.

Lee, Stan. *Stan Lee's How to Draw Comics.* New York: Watson-Guptill, 2010.

McNab, Chris. *Mythical Monsters: The Scariest Creatures from Legends, Books, and Movies.* Lake Mary, FL: Tangerine Press, 2006.

Web Sites

Due to the changing nature of Internet links, PowerKids Press has developed an online list of Web sites related to the subject of this book. This site is updated regularly. Please use this link to access the list:

www.powerkidslinks.com/hdgn/villain/

INDEX